AUDIO EFFECTS, MIXING AND MASTERING

METIN BEKTAS

DEDICATION

This book is dedicated to my family.

CONTENTS

1. Audio Effects And Automation

1.1. Compressors

Small is the new big.
(Seth Godin)

Almost all music and recorded speech that you hear has been sent through at least one compressor at some point during the production process. If you are serious about music production, you need to get familiar with this powerful tool. This means understanding the big picture as well as getting to know each of the parameters (Threshold, Ratio, Attack, Release, Make-Up Gain) intimately.

- **How They Work**

Throughout any song the volume level varies over time. It might hover around - 6 dB in the verse, rise to - 2 dB in the first chorus, drop to - 8 dB in the interlude, and so on. A term that is worth knowing in this context is the dynamic range. It refers to the difference in volume level from the softest to the loudest part. Some genres of music, such as orchestral music, generally have a large dynamic range, while for mainstream pop and rock a much smaller dynamic range is desired. A symphony might range from - 20 dB in the soft oboe solo to - 2 dB for the exciting final chord (dynamic range: 18 dB), whereas your common pop song will rather go from - 8 dB in the first verse to 0 dB in the last chorus (dynamic range: 8 dB).

During a recording we have some control over what dynamic range we will end up with. We can tell the musicians to take it easy in the verse and really go for it in the chorus. But of course this is not very accurate and we'd like to have full control of the dynamic range rather than just some. We'd also like to be able to to change the dynamic range later on. Compressors make this (and much more) possible.

The compressor constantly monitors the volume level. As long as the level is below a certain **threshold**, the compressor will not do anything. Only when the level exceeds the threshold does it become active and dampen the excess volume by a certain **ratio**. In short: everything below the threshold stays as it is, everything above the threshold gets compressed. Keep this in mind.

Suppose for example we set the threshold to - 10 dB and the ratio to 4:1. Before applying the compressor, our song varies from a minimum value of - 12 dB in the verse to a maximum value - 2 dB in the chorus. Let's look at the verse first. Here the volume does not exceed the threshold and thus the compressor does not spring into action. The signal will pass through unchanged. The story is different for the chorus. Its volume level is 8 dB above the threshold. The compressor takes this excess volume and dampens it according to the ratio we set. To be more specific: the compressor turns the 8 dB excess volume into a mere 8 dB / 4 = 2 dB. So the compressed song ranges from - 12 dB in the verse to -10 dB + 2 dB = - 8 dB in the chorus.

Here's a summary of the process:

Settings:

Threshold: - 10 dB

Ratio: 4:1

3

Before:

- Minimum: - 12 dB

- Maximum: - 2 dB

- Dynamic range: 10 dB

Excess volume (threshold to maximum): 8 dB

With ratio applied: 8 dB / 4 = 2 dB

After:

- Minimum: - 12 dB

- Maximum: - 8 dB

- Dynamic range: 4 dB ⅃

As you can see, the compressor had a significant effect on the dynamic range. Choosing appropriate values for the threshold and ratio, we are free to compress the song to any dynamic range we desire. When using a DAW (Digital Audio Workstation such as Cubase, FL Studio or Ableton Live), it is possible to see the workings of a compressor with your own eyes. The image below shows the uncompressed file (top) and the compressed file (bottom) with the threshold set to - 12 dB and the ratio to 2:1.

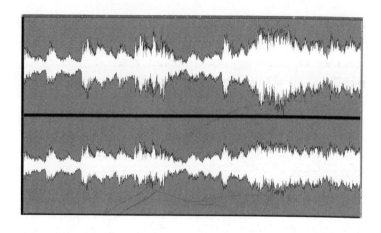

The soft parts are identical, while the louder parts (including the short and possibly problematic peaks) have been reduced in volume. The dynamic range clearly shrunk in the process. Note that after applying the compressor, the song's effective volume (RMS) is much lower. Since this is usually not desired, most compressors have a parameter called **make-up gain**. Here you can specify by how much you'd like the compressor to raise the volume of the song after the compression process is finished. This increase in volume is applied to all parts of the song, soft or loud, so there will not be another change in the dynamic range. It only makes up for the loss in loudness (hence the name).

- **Usage of Compressors**

We already got to know one application of the compressor: controlling the dynamic range of a song. But usually this is just a first step in reaching another goal: increasing the effective volume of the song. Suppose you have a song with a dynamic range of 10 dB and you want to make it as loud as possible. So you move the volume fader until the maximum level is at 0 dB. According to the dynamic range, the minimum level will now be at - 10 dB. The effective volume will obviously be somewhere in-between the two values. For the sake of simplicity, we'll assume it to be right in the middle, at - 5 dB. But this is too soft for your taste. What to do?

You insert a compressor with a threshold of - 6 dB and a ratio of 3:1. The 4 dB range from the minimum level - 10 dB to the threshold - 6 dB is unchanged, while the 6 dB range from the threshold - 6 dB to the maximum level 0 dB is compressed to 6 dB / 3 = 2 dB. So overall the dynamic range is reduced to 4 dB + 2 dB = 6 dB. Again you move the volume fader until the maximum volume level coincides with 0 dB. However, this time the minimum volume will be higher, at - 6 dB, and the effective volume at - 3 dB (up from the - 5 dB we started with). Mission accomplished, the combination of compression and gain indeed left us with a higher average volume.

In theory, this means we can get the effective volume up to almost any value we desire by compressing a song and then making it louder. We could have the whole song close to 0 dB. This possibility has led to a "loudness war" in music production. Why not go along with that? For one, you always want to put as much emphasis as possible on the hook. This is hard to do if the intro and verse is already blaring at maximum volume. Another reason is that severely reducing the dynamic range kills the expressive elements in your song. It is not a coincidence that music which strongly relies on expressive elements (orchestral and acoustic music) usually has the highest dynamic range. It needs the wide range to go from expressing peaceful serenity to expressing destructive desperation. Read the following out loud and memorize it: the more expression it has, the less you should compress. While a techno song might work at maximum volume, a ballad sure won't.

Background Info - SPL and Loudness

Talking about how loud something is can be surprisingly complicated. The problem is that our brain does not process sound inputs in a linear fashion. A sound wave with twice the sound pressure does not necessarily seem twice as loud to us. So when expressing how loud something is, we can either do this by using well-defined physical quantities such as the sound pressure level (which unfortunately does not reflect how loud a person perceives something to be) or by using subjective psycho-acoustic quantities such as loudness (which is hard to define and measure properly).

Sound waves are pressure and density fluctuations that propagate at a material- and temperature-dependent speed in a medium. For air at 20 °C this speed is roughly 340 m/s. The quantity sound pressure expresses the deviation of the sound wave pressure from the pressure of the surrounding air. The sound pressure level, in short: SPL, is proportional to the logarithm of the effective sound pressure. Long story short: the stronger the sound pressure, the higher the SPL. The SPL is used to objectively measure how loud something is. Another important objective quantity for this purpose is the volume. It is a measure of how much energy is contained in an audio signal and thus closely related to the SPL.

A subjective quantity that reflects how loud we perceive something to be is loudness. Due to our highly non-linear brains, the loudness of an audio signal is not simply proportional to its SPL or volume level. Rather, loudness depends in a complex way on the SPL, frequency, duration of the sound, its bandwidth, etc ... In the image below you can see an approximation of the relationship between loudness, SPL and frequency.

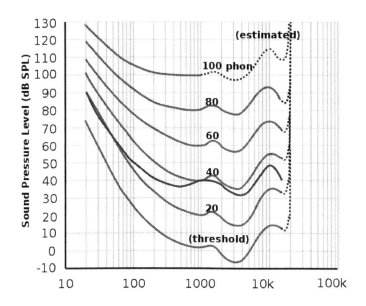

Any red curve is a curve of equal loudness. Here's how we can read the chart. Take a look at the red curve at the very bottom. It starts at 75 dB SPL and a frequency of 20 Hz and reaches 25 dB SPL at 100 Hz. Since the red curve is a curve of equal loudness, we can conclude we perceive a 75 dB SPL sound at 20 Hz to be just as loud as a 25 dB SPL sound at 100 Hz, even though from a purely physical point of view the first sound is three times as loud as the second one (75 dB / 25 dB = 3).

(Compressor in Cubase)

- **Threshold and Ratio**

What's the ideal threshold to use? This depends on what you are trying to accomplish. Suppose you set the threshold at a relatively high value (for example - 10 dB in a good mix). In this case the compressor will be inactive for most of the song and only kick in during the hook and short peaks. With the threshold set to a high value, you are thus "taking the top off". This would be a suitable choice if you are happy with the dynamics in general, but would like to make the mix less aggressive.

What about low thresholds (such as -25 dB in a good mix)? In this case the compressor will be active for the most part of the song and will make the entire song quite dense. This is something to consider if you aim to really push the loudness of the song. Once the mix is dense, you can go for a high effective volume. But a low threshold compression can also add warmth to a ballad, so it's not necessarily a tool restricted to usage in the loudness war.

Onto the ratio. If you set the ratio to a high value (such as 5:1 and higher), you are basically telling the mix: to the threshold and no further. Anything past the threshold will be heavily compressed, which is great if you have pushy peaks that make a mix overly aggressive. This could be the result of a snare that's way too loud or an inexperienced singer. Whatever the cause, a carefully chosen threshold and a high ratio should take care of it in a satisfying manner. Note though that in this case the compressor should be applied to the track that is causing the problem and not the entire mix.

A low value for the ratio (such as 2:1 or smaller) will have a rather subtle effect. Such values are perfect if you want to apply the compressor to a mix that already sounds well and just needs a finishing touch. The mix will become a little more dense, but its character will be kept intact.

- **Attack and Release**

There are two important parameters we have ignored so far: the attack and release. The **attack** parameter allows you to specify how quickly the compressor sets in once the volume level goes past the threshold. A compressor with a long attack (20 milliseconds or more) will let short peaks pass. As long as these peaks are not over-the-top, this is not necessarily a bad thing. The presence of short peaks, also called transients, is important for a song's liveliness and natural sound. A long attack makes sure that these qualities are preserved and that the workings of the compressor are less noticeable.

A short attack (5 milliseconds or less) can produce a beautifully crisp sound that is suitable for energetic music. But it is important to note that if the attack is too short, the compressor will kill the transients and the whole mix will sound flat and bland. Even worse, a short attack can lead to clicks and a nervous "pumping effect". Be sure to watch out for those as you shorten the attack.

The **release** is the time for the compressor to become inactive once the volume level goes below the threshold. It is usually much longer than the attack, but the overall principles are similar. A long release (600 milliseconds or more) will make sure that the compression happens in a more subtle fashion, while a short release (150 milliseconds or less) can produce a pumping sound.

It is always a good idea to choose the release so that it fits the rhythm of your song (the same of course is true for temporal parameters in reverb and delay). One way to do this is to calculate the time per beat TPB in milliseconds from your song's tempo, as measured in beats per minute BPM, and use this value as the point of reference.

$$TPB\ [ms] = 60000\ /\ BPM$$

For example, in a song with the tempo BPM = 120 the duration of one beat is TPB = 60000 / 120 = 500 ms. If you need a longer release, use a multiple of it (1000 ms, 1500 ms, and so on), for a shorter release divide it by any natural number (500 ms / 2 = 250 ms, 500 ms / 3 = 167 ms, and so on). This way the compressor will "breathe" in unison with your music.

If you are not sure where to start regarding attack and release, just make use of the 20/200-rule: Set the attack to 20 ms, the release to 200 ms and work towards the ideal values from there. Alternatively, you can always go through the presets of the compressor to find suitable settings.

- **Parallel Compression**

Parallel compression is an advanced compression technique that will give you the "best of both worlds". It allows you to produce the dense sound so characteristic for compressors without giving up too much of the track's dynamics and transients. Start by duplicating the track. Leave the original track as it is and place a compressor on the duplicate track. Set the the compressor's ratio to a moderate value (for example 2.5:1), choose a short attack of several milliseconds and a release of around 300 milliseconds. Play both tracks and set the volume faders to your liking.

How is this better than simply compressing the track? We already noted that a compressor will limit the dynamic range of a track and kill some (if the attack is too short even all) transients. By keeping one of the tracks in its original form, we make sure that there's no danger of losing the dynamics and the liveliness of the song.

You can think of parallel compression as a way of applying the compressor at a certain percentage. For example, if both tracks have an equal volume level after we compressed one of it, we basically applied the compressor at 50 %. By moving the volume faders you are free to choose to what degree the compression should take place. If you feel that the track is missing too much of its natural sound, you can simply move the volume fader of the unaltered track up. If you want a denser sound, you do the opposite. So you are left with an additional (invisible) compression parameter to optimize your sound.

- **Multi-Band Compressors**

Up to now, whenever I used the word compressor I actually referred to the single-band compressor. But many DAWs also give you the option of using an even more powerful compression tool: the multi-band compressor. It looks quite intimidating at first, but taking a closer look you will come to realize that you know most of its parameters already. So no need to panic.

(Multi-Band Compressor in Cubase)

The multi-band compressor consists of a number of single-band compressors (usually four) that are all limited to a certain bandwidth. For example, compressor number one only analyzes and alters the portion of your music that is between 16 and 150 Hz. Compressor number two covers all frequencies from 150 Hz to 1000 Hz. And so on. So each single-band compressor is given its own territory and rules it with the parameters you are already familiar with: threshold, ratio, attack and release.

In most multi-band compressors you are free to choose the frequency ranges, so the following bands are just for guidance. To get familiar with the bands, make sure to use the compressor's solo function (which in the above picture is just below the input-output diagram on the right side). Soloing the bands is very instructive even if you don't end up using the multi-band compressor.

Commonly the lowest band spans from 16 Hz to 150 Hz (bass) and contains the sub-bass, low rumbling noises, kick-bass and the fundamental notes of the bass instruments. This range is the essential foundation of any song, but too much of it can cause the music to become boomy very quickly. The next band usually covers all frequencies from 150 Hz to around 1500 Hz (lower midrange) and you can find the overtones of the bass in it as well as the fundamental notes of all the melodic instruments: vocals, guitars, strings, pads, and so on. Here lies the warmth and fullness of your song, but over-emphasizing it will produce a muddy sound.

The third band usually goes from 1500 Hz to 5000 Hz (upper midrange) and contains the overtones of all the melodic instruments as well as much of the hi-hat and cymbal action. The band's sound can range from bright at best to tinny and penetrating at worst. All that's left is the "air" between 5000 Hz and 20000 Hz (treble). Here you'll find the remaining overtones of the instruments and the high end of the hi-hats, cymbals and vocals. This band will give the song a brilliant sound, but can be noisy and piercing if too loud.

There are several reasons why a multi-band compressor is superior to its single-band counterpart. When a single-band compressor springs into action, it compresses the mix across the entire frequency spectrum. This means for example that a peaking bass can cause higher notes, that are at an appropriate volume, to be dampened as well, making the mix more boomy. A multi-band compressor on the other hand will only compress the bass peak and leave the higher regions unchanged, keeping the original character of the mix.

The more surgical multi-band compression tool can also help to establish spectral balance. This is especially helpful for audio production beginners who might not notice that there's a "frequency jam" in the lower midrange, something that quickly happens without proper EQing of the individual tracks. With too many instruments overlapping in the lower midrange band, the mix will sound rather muddy. A multi-band compressor with the right settings will alleviate (but not fix) this problem and create a more balanced frequency distribution.

The multi-band compressor can also be used as a dynamic EQ. Are the cymbals or the singer's sibilant consonants ("s", "z" and "sh") getting too loud in the chorus? One way of tackling this problem would be to lower the frequencies around 5000 Hz with a common EQ. But unfortunately, the EQ would dampen these frequencies not only in the chorus, but also in all other parts of the song, sort of like fixing a scratch on your car with a hammer. You got rid of the scratch, but caused a lot more damage in doing it. Applying a multi-band compressor here with a well-chosen band around 5000 Hz (while bypassing the other three bands) would be a much better solution. It will only dampen the band if it gets too loud, that is, in the chorus. The verses get to keep their original sound. Most DeEssers work like this.

As you can see, the multi-band compressor is worth studying. Don't be intimidated by its look and start experimenting with it. Solo the bands to see what's in there, load all the presets to see how this will impact your music and apply what you learned about the single-band compressor to the compressors in the multi-band version. I'm sure you won't end up regretting it.

In A Nutshell - Compressors

- *Compressors reduce the dynamic range of a song by dampening all sounds above the threshold. The ratio determines how pronounced the dampening is.*

- *Moderate values for the threshold and ratio make a song denser and warmer without restricting the dynamics too strongly.*

- *Longer attack and release times make the workings of the compressor less noticeable and prevent "pumping".*

- *The parallel compression technique allows you to apply a compressor partly to a track.*

- *Multi-band compressors allow you to compress isolated frequency bands. They can help to establish spectral balance and act as dynamic equalizers.*

1.2. Limiters

Extreme remedies are very appropriate for extreme diseases.
(Hippocrates)

Limiters are closely related to compressors. To be specific, a limiter is a compressor with the highest ratio possible (∞:1) and an extremely short attack. A ratio of "infinity-to-one" just means that every note louder than the threshold is pushed down to the threshold. Hence the volume will never go past the threshold, no matter what. Keep in mind that in limiters the threshold is sometimes simply called output.

What other parameters can you find in a typical limiter besides the threshold? Since it is a compressor, you are still free to choose the release. Moderate values for the release are around 200 ms, for drums it can go as low as 0.1 ms. Often a better sound is achieved by using the "auto" function rather than setting the release yourself. Another parameter you commonly find is the gain (sometimes just called input). It specifies by how much the volume of the mix is increased or decreased before it goes through the limiter.

(Limiter in Cubase)

What's the point of this extreme form of compression? Since all louder parts are pushed down to the threshold, the limiter acts as a "brick wall". It is thus perfect for protecting the mix from clipping. If you are using the limiter for this purpose, make sure that it is the last effect in line. If you set a limiter and then work on the EQ or include reverb after that, your mix could still become subject to clipping.

Another application of the limiter is to increase the effective volume of a song. This can be done by choosing a large gain and a threshold close to 0 dB. Below you can see an example of this. The gain / input is set to 12 dB (so the volume level of the mix is increased by 12 dB before it goes into the limiter) and the threshold / output set to -0.3 dB (so the volume level will never go past this value).

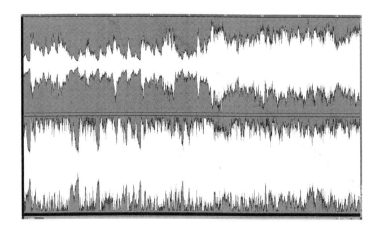

If used wisely, this can increase the average volume considerably while still maintaining the illusion of a large dynamic range (which is what a common compressor is not able to do). If overdone, the result will be a blaring and flat mix that hardly deserves the name music. It is up to your ears and brain to find the right settings.

In A Nutshell - Limiters

- *Limiters are compressors with an extremely short attack and infinite-to-one ratio.*

- *They can be used as a final insert to prevent clipping and to increase the effective volume level.*

1.3. Equalizers

A problem is a chance for you to do your best.
(Duke Ellington)

Equalizers are to audio engineers as screwdrivers are to mechanics - a fundamental tool you'll need for any job. As you start your journey into mixing and mastering, learn as much as you can about equalization, from the big picture to the nuances. This approach will most certainly pay off later on.

The task of the EQ is to boost or cut a certain frequency region to either solve a problem or make a mix shine. If the song is too boomy, a cut around 100 Hz can do wonders, if it's missing warmth, a boost around 300 Hz might be just what it needs. To properly use the EQ, you have to be able to pick up such problems and shortcomings, identify the corresponding frequency region and take the appropriate action. The latter requires you to know the parameters of your equalizer, which is why we start the chapter by looking at different types of equalizers and the parameters you'll find in them.

- **Graphic EQs**

A very intuitive equalization tool is the graphic EQ. It allows you to specify the **gain** (the applied boost or cut as measured in decibels) using sliders at fixed **center frequencies**. The great thing about them is that they are easy to use and that it just takes one quick peek to have the complete picture of how your song's spectrum is modified. But there's also a downside to this. The fact that the center frequencies are fixed and that you have no (or at least not full) control over the bandwidth of the boost or cut takes away some flexibility and precision.

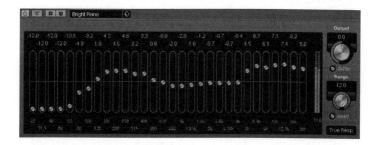

(30-Band Graphic EQ in Cubase)

Note that the graphic EQ is defined by having control over the gain at fixed center frequencies and not by the presence of a graphical interface as the name might suggest. There are a lot of EQs with a graphical interface that do not belong in the graphic EQ category.

- **Semi-Parametric EQs**

Semi-parametric EQs take the equalization concept a step further. Additionally to the gain, you are also free to set the center frequencies. They are much rarer than the graphic EQs or their more flexible brothers, the parametric EQs.

(Semi-Parametric Bass EQ. Top: Frequency Knob, Bottom: Gain Knob)

- **Parametric EQs**

Parametric EQs give the user the greatest precision possible. Besides the gain and the center frequency, they allow you to alter the bandwidth of the bell-shaped "incision" via the so-called **Q factor**. A small Q-value will result in a large bandwidth (broad bell curve), while a large Q-value leads to a small bandwidth (narrow bell curve). To be more specific, the bandwidth B of the boost or cut is the ratio of center frequency f to the Q factor:

B = f / Q

Which bandwidth is optimal depends on the purpose of the incision. If there's a problem with the kick bass, a narrow bell curve around 100 Hz should deal with it in a satisfying manner, while for sweetening the mix during mastering a broader (less noticeable) bell curve is much more suitable.

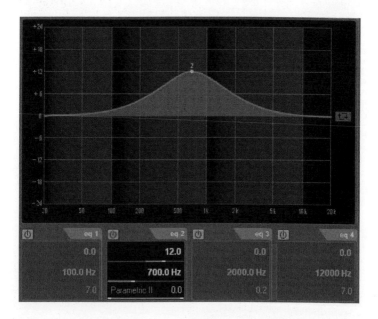

(4-Band Parametric EQ in Cubase. Small Q, High Gain Boost)

- **Shelving EQs**

Shelving EQs replace the bell curve with a plateau boost or cut. The form of the plateau is determined by the gain, transition frequency and Q factor. In this case the Q factor specifies the bandwidth of the transition from initial level to plateau level rather than the size of the incision. Many parametric EQs (especially the digital ones) include a shelving EQ.

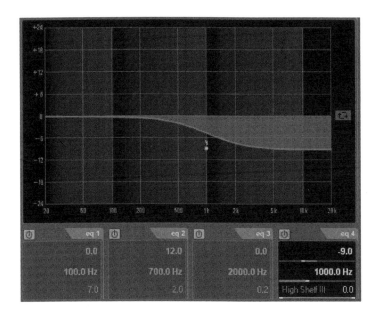

(Small Q, High Gain Plateau Cut in Cubase's Parametric EQ)

- **Filter EQs**

Filter EQs (or simply: filters) force a straight-line cut onto a song's spectrum. Filters that cut out low frequencies, are called highpass filters (as only high frequencies are allowed to pass) while those that cut out high frequencies are referred to as lowpass filters. The most important parameters for filtering are the **cut-off frequency** and the gain, which controls the steepness of the cut.

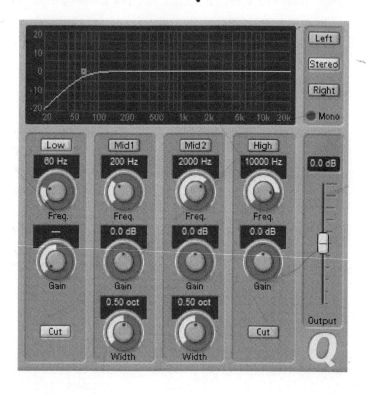

(Filter Plugin in Cubase)

- **Using Equalizers**

As already mentioned, EQs are used for two purposes 1) to solve specific problems with the audio such as a boomy bass or an overly aggressive snare and 2) to spice up a mix. It's important to note that it's a common beginner's mistake to choose extreme values for the gain. If you are working with relatively good tracks, there should never be a reason to set the gain higher than 6 dB (or better yet, 3 dB). Anything beyond that will create a severe imbalance in the song's spectrum and sound very artificial. If the problem at hand cannot be fixed with a gain below 6 dB, the only sensible decision is to go back to the recording phase.

Before you start working with an EQ, make sure to have an overview over the frequency ranges of the instruments in your mix. Take the time to memorize the ones most important to you, as you will need this information over and over. The range can be divided into the **fundamental region** (this is where the fundamental notes of the instrument lie), the **harmonic region** (this is where the most noticeable overtones are) and the **air** (containing the remaining overtones). The air is not included in the table. It usually spans from the from the end of the harmonic region all the way up to 16.000 Hz and is rarely audible.

Instrument	Fundamentals	Harmonics
Male Vocals	100 - 900 Hz	900 - 8.000 Hz
Female Vocals	200 - 1.100 Hz	1.100 - 8.000 Hz
Kick	50 - 500 Hz	500 - 8.000 Hz
Toms	70 - 500 Hz	500 - 3.000 Hz
Snare	100 - 300 Hz	300 - 10.000 Hz
Cymbals[1]	300 - 900 Hz	900 - 16.000 Hz
Bass	40 - 300 Hz	300 - 5.000 Hz
Guitar	80 - 1.200 Hz	1.200 - 5.000 Hz
String Section[2]	40 - 1.300 Hz	1.300 Hz - 16.000 Hz

[1] Also produce a clang between 200 - 300 Hz

[2] Including one or more c-basses

Background Info - Harmonics

In theory, hitting the middle C on a piano should produce a sound wave with a frequency of 523.25 Hz and nothing else. However, running the resulting audio through a spectrum analyzer, it becomes obvious that there's much more going on. This is true for all other instruments, from tubas to trumpets, basoons to flutes, c-basses to violins. Play any note and you'll get a package of sound waves at different frequencies rather than just one.

First of all: why is that? Let's focus on stringed instruments. When you pluck the string, it goes into its most basic vibration mode: it moves up and down as a whole at a certain frequency f. This is the so called first harmonic (or fundamental). But shortly after that, the nature of the vibration changes and the string enters a second mode: while one half of the string moves up, the other half moves down. This happens naturally and is just part of the string's dynamics. In this mode, called the second harmonic, the vibration accelerates to a frequency of $2 \cdot f$. The story continues in this fashion as other modes of vibration appear: the third harmonic at a frequency $3 \cdot f$, the fourth harmonic at $4 \cdot f$, and so on.

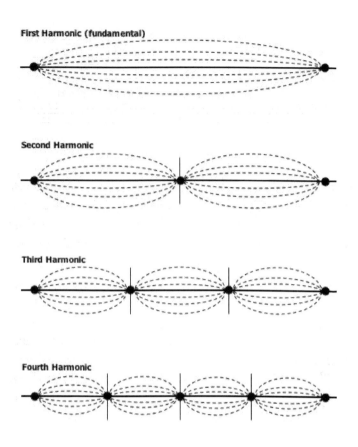

A note is determined by the frequency. As already stated, the middle C on the piano should produce a sound wave with a frequency of 523.25 Hz. And indeed it does produce said sound wave, but it is only the first harmonic. As the string continues to vibrate, all the other harmonics follow, producing overtones. In the image below you can see which notes you'll get when playing a C:

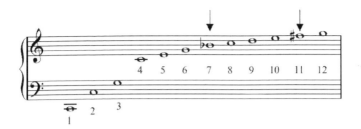

Quite the package! And note that the major chord is fully included within the first four overtones. So it's buy a note, get a chord free. You might wonder why it is that we don't seem to perceive the additional notes. Well, we do and we don't. We don't perceive the overtones consciously because the amplitude, and thus volume, of each harmonic is smaller than the amplitude of the previous one (however, this is a rule of thumb and exceptions are possible as any instrument will emphasize some overtones in particular). But I can assure you that when listening to a digitally produced note, you'll feel that something's missing. It will sound bland and cold. So unconsciously, we do perceive and desire the overtones.

If there's a certain problem you'd like to take care of and you don't seem to be able to locate the appropriate frequency with the help of the above frequency range table, try the **sweeping technique**. Use the EQ to make narrow, maximum gain boost. Move the resulting bell curve through the spectrum until the problem becomes very pronounced. The displayed center frequency is the frequency you where looking for.

The sweeping technique is also an excellent method for locating and eliminating **resonances.** As you sweep through an instrument's sound, you will notice that at certain frequencies a piercing ringing noise appears. These are resonances and removing them consequently with narrow cuts will bring out the best in your tracks.

Whenever working with the EQ, try to **imagine the impact of a boost or cut** before you activate it. This is a great technique for training both your ears and mind. The more you'll do it, the quicker and more precise you'll be able to identify where a mix needs a boost or cut to really shine.

- **Quick Tips**

To complete the section on equalizers, here are a few quick tips that you might find helpful when mixing and mastering your next song. However, don't apply them blindly. Use them only when necessary and be sure to check if they produce the result you were hoping for.

- If the **vocals are hard to understand**, a boost between 2 - 6 kHz might be just what you need.

- For **more intimacy in your vocal track**, run it through a DeEsser and include a high frequency shelf starting at 10 kHz.

- Does your **guitar sound dull**? You should have changed your old strings before recording. To get that new string sound in post, boost from 6 - 12 kHz.

- If the **electric guitar lacks in sharpness or is too aggressive**, boost or cut the region 2 - 4 kHz.

- Is there too little clarity in the high frequency range? This might be a result of the **guitar harmonics getting in the way of the cymbals**. Boost the guitar at 6 kHz and cut the cymbals there, cut the guitar at 10 kHz and boost the cymbals there.

- You might have to sacrifice the low frequencies of your guitars, snare and vocals to achieve a **clear mix**. The low-cut leaves space for the bass and kick.

- Is the **bass and kick turning your mix into mud**? Then try a cut around 300 Hz.

- If your mix is too boomy, there might be **a conflict between the bass and kick**. Boost the kick at around 80 Hz and cut the bass there. For an even better separation, boost the bass at 250 Hz and cut the kick there.

- Below 40 Hz, there's nothing except **rumbling** from heating, ventilation, traffic, etc ... It might not be audible, but it still uses up precious dynamic space. Get rid of it mercilessly, don't leave survivors.

- Our ears are most sensitive between 3 - 4 kHz. So if you want to **make an instrument stand out**, this is where to boost it. Cut conflicting instruments in the same range for an even more pronounced effect.

As you noticed, a lot of these tips focus on making space. This is a very central part of mixing. If you want a clear mix, you have to make sacrifices. You have a lot of instruments, but only one bass band and only one 3 - 4 kHz range. Think about which instruments get the top spots.

In A Nutshell - Equalizers

- *Equalizers allow you to boost or cut specific frequency bands for individual instruments or an entire mix.*

- *To be able to use EQs properly, get familiar with the frequency ranges of the instruments in your music.*

- *To identify at which frequency a certain problem is located, use the sweeping technique.*

- *Always imagine the impact of your boost or cut before applying it. This is great training for your ears.*

- *Use the EQ to get rid of resonances and low-end rumbling as well as to make space in certain bands. The latter is vital for a clear mix.*

1.4. Reverb and Delay

Your mind powers will not work on me, boy.
(Jabba the Hutt)

Reverb is among the most often used (and misused) effects in audio production. It can make a flat recording sound grand and really glue a mix together. Too much of it however will turn a good mix into a muddy or boomy mess - a typical beginner's mistake. Try your best to avoid this trap.

- **Reverb and Delay**

Before we go any further, let's make sure we understand the difference between reverb and delay. From a physical point of view, they are one and the same, that is, a result of sound waves being reflected from walls or other barriers. The difference rather comes from how our brain processes sound.

Suppose you are in a room and produce a sound by snapping your fingers. The sound waves you created travel to the walls and are reflected back to you. This happens in a very short time span as sound waves travel very fast - with roughly 330 meters per second or 33 centimeters (circa one foot) per millisecond. So in a commonly sized bedroom the first reflection will reach you after only 5 milliseconds. The sound waves keep on traveling back and forth within the room while dissipating.

Our brain has a curious way of processing reflections that arrive within the first 30 milliseconds after producing the sound. Instead of distinctly perceiving those early reflections, the brain blends them with the sound source. It will even tell you that these reflections came from the same place as the original sound. So to us it seems that the original sound persist. This Jedi mind-trick is called reverb (or hall).

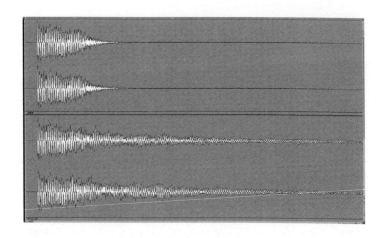

(Top: Dry Snare, Bottom: Snare with Reverb)

The reflections that arrive at your location after the initial 30 milliseconds are perceived as distinct reflections coming from the walls. They go by the name delay (or echo). A good example is a mountain throwing back your "hello". The reflection is heard as a distinct sound originating from the mountain and is not blended with your original "hello".

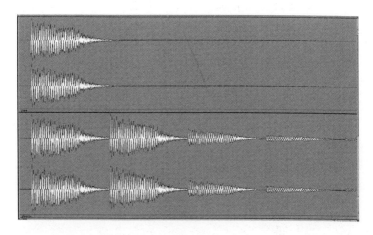

(Top: Dry Snare, Bottom: Snare with Delay)

- **Reverb Time**

What are the common parameters you find in a reverb plugin? There's a great variety of reverb plugins out there, some very similar, others very unique. But all will feature a parameter called **reverb time** (also called decay or RT60). It specifies the time it takes the reverberation to decay by 60 dB or in short: how long the reverb persists. Obviously this quantity is related to the size of a room. The bigger it is, the longer the reverb time will be.

At the end of the 19th century, Wallace Clement Sabine empirically studied the reverb time at Harvard University and derived a handy approximation formula for it. Here is a modified version of it that takes into account air dissipation:

$$T = \frac{0.16 \cdot V}{a \cdot A + b \cdot V}$$

with T being the reverb time in seconds, V the room's volume in cubic-meters and A the surface area of the room in square-meters. For common brickwork and plaster walls the absorption coefficient is about a = 0.03, for wood a = 0.3 and for acoustic tiles it can go as high as a = 0.8. As for the air absorption coefficient, it is roughly b = 0.02 at 50 % humidity. Keep in mind though that the formula is only valid for empty rooms. Having sound absorbers such as equipment and people in a room can greatly reduce the reverb time (that's right, I just called you a sound absorber, what are you gonna do about it?).

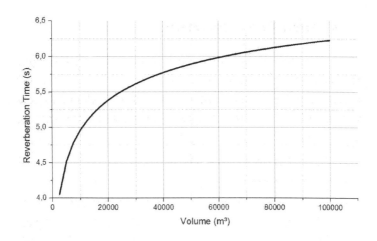

(Variation Of Reverb Time With Volume For Empty, Rectangular Rooms)

If you don't like formulas, don't worry. The formula, while good to know, is not essential for music production. Just keep in mind some reference values for the reverb time: 0.5 s for small rooms in a home, 1 s for churches, 1.5 s for concert halls, 2 s for small arenas and 2.5 s for large arenas.

(Reverb Plugin in Cubase)

- **Other Reverb Parameters**

Another parameter that is found in almost all reverb plugins is the **pre-delay.** It is the time span between the sound being created and the arrival of the first reflection. Calculating it is very simple. If the closest wall is at a distance of d meters, then the pre-delay t in milliseconds is roughly:

$$t = 6 \cdot d$$

Just like the reverb time, the pre-delay generally grows with the size of the room. Hence, it's a good idea to set the pre-delay in a more or less proportional fashion to the reverb time. Assuming you are in the middle of the room, typical pre-delays are around 20 ms for small rooms in a home, 60 ms for a church, 120 ms for a concert hall, 200 ms for a small arena and 250 ms for a large arena.

Combining a small pre-delay and large reverb time is also possible from a physical point of view. This combination occurs for example in a long tunnel or near a wall in a large room. In both cases the first reflection will come back quickly, while the size of the room guarantees a long reverb time.

Another important parameter you can commonly find in reverb plugins is **diffusion**. Suppose you are in a house with two rooms of identical size. The rooms only differ in surface texture: while one room has a perfectly smooth surface, the surface of the other room is very rough. Because of the equal size, the reverb time and pre-delay will be the same in both rooms. But despite that, the reverb will sound different. While the smooth surface in the one room creates a harder and more noticeable reverb, the rough surface in the other room will spawn a warmer and more subtle reverb. The diffusion parameter allows you to simulate this situation. Set it close to 0 % for a smooth surface (hard reverb) and close to 100 % for a rough surface (warm reverb).

Also very helpful is the parameter **mix**. With it you specify how much of the wet signal, that is, the signal that was processed by the reverb plugin, you'd like to have in the output. If it's close to 0 % the reverb will hardly be noticeable, while a value of 100 % gives you the full dose of reverb. When choosing your value, don't forget the saying "less is more" A mix of around 10 % is often quite sufficient (if the reverb is used as an insert - more on that later).

What else will there be in the reverb plugin? This can vary greatly. Many plugins also a include a **filter** and this for good reasons. Dampening low and high frequencies before having the reverb plugin process your signal makes a lot of sense. Low frequency audio content can easily make a mix boomy and muddy when run through a reverb plugin. And having a lot of high frequencies in your reverb sounds very unnatural. Why is that? Air has the habit of dampening high frequencies much more strongly than low frequencies as it transmits sound waves. So when the sound that was reflected back and forth reaches you, the air has already taken out a lot of the high frequencies. Hence, natural reverb lacks in high frequency content.

The filters are usually controlled by a cut-off and dampening parameter. The cut-off parameter determines at what frequency to start dampening the spectrum (usually somewhere around 50 Hz for the low cut and 7000 Hz for the high cut). In Cubase's Roomworks plugin the cut-off parameters for the filters can be found on the left side at the top. The dampening parameter, usually in form of a gain knob, specifies how pronounced the cut is. Moderate values are around - 4 dB. In the Roomworks plugin the dampening parameters are located on the left side at the bottom.

- **Delay Parameters**

(Mono Delay Plugin in Cubase)

The most important parameter in delay plugins is the delay, that is, the time between reflections in milliseconds. Note that while for compressors and reverb plugins setting the temporal parameters to fit the rhythm of your song is a neat trick to achieve a more perfect sound, in case of delay making a careful choice is essential. An out-of-sync delay can turn a mix into a mess, which is why most delay plugins feature a sync function that you should make use of.

The feedback parameter controls the number of reflections as well as their intensity. A value close to 0 % will only produce one noticeable reflection (the following reflections decay too quickly to be heard), while a value close to 100 % will add a long line of noticeable reflections to each note.

- **Using Reverb And Delay**

The possibilities of using reverb and delay in your mix are endless. Be bold and experiment with them. Besides a few things to keep in mind, there's no right and wrong. In other words: if it sounds good, it is good. What's to keep in mind? For one, reverb or delay on low frequency audio content often leads to a dark and boomy mix. Watch out for that when adding them to the bass, kick, cello, viola and guitar.

If having a relatively heavy reverb on the guitar is important for your song, make sure to cut the low frequencies beforehand, either with the EQ or the filter included in the reverb plugin. If the guitar sounds too thin in solo after the low cut, don't worry. It's not about how it sounds solo, it's all about how it sounds within the mix. As for the bass, it's almost always better off with very little or no reverb. If you'd like to have a more vivid bass, why not add some distortion instead?

Problems can also occur in the high frequency range, especially in case of vocal tracks. A heavy reverb or delay can make sibilant consonants even more problematic. Considering that the vocals are always at the front of a song, this can ruin an otherwise great mix. So if you want to put a noticeable reverb on the vocals (which is generally a good idea), make sure to place a DeEsser before the reverb plugin.

A more obvious point that you should keep in mind is to use the same reverb room (or comparable rooms) for the majority of the tracks in your mix. For specific elements such as the vocals or electric guitar you can and should deviate from this rule. There's nothing more powerful than an epic cathedral guitar solo over a small room mix - try it out.

Reverb and delay are great tools to create a sense of depth in your mix. So before you start applying them, think about which of your tracks are close and which are far from the audience. The farther back an instrument is, the higher the value of the mix parameter should be. You can boost this sense of depth by making a more pointed high cut for the instruments in the back (remember, if sound travels a greater distance in air, it will lose more of the high frequency content). A typical set-up for a rock song is: vocals and solo instruments in the front, guitars and drums in the middle, everything else in the back (especially strings and pads).

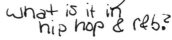
what is it in hip hop & r&b?

- **Insert or Send?**

An insert effect is any effect that is placed directly into the path of one track. This is the most intuitive way of putting an effect on a track and if you're a beginner you've probably been only using insert effects up to now. You simply open the track's settings and include the effect. Done and done. For many purposes, this is quite sufficient.

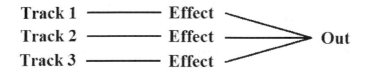

Track 1 ——————— **Effect**
Track 2 ——————— **Effect** ——————▶ **Out**
Track 3 ——————— **Effect**

(Signal Paths Using Insert-Effects)

Using an effect as a send means making a short a detour. Instead of including the effect in the track's path, we send the signal of the track to the effect, which is then sent to the output. So the original signal and the signal processed by the effect plugin are separated. Both are ultimately send to the output and with the respective volume faders you can determine how much of each you'd like to have in the output. [Instead of turning up the mix parameter to get more reverb on a track, you turn up the volume of the separate effect channel]

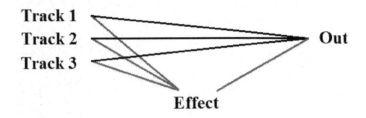

(Signal Paths Using A Send-Effect)

What's the point of all this hassle? On the one hand there's the economic side of it. Routing ten tracks to the separate effect channel requires a lot less computing power than inserting one and the same reverb on all ten tracks individually. Your computer will thank you for that. More importantly, [you are now free to put effects on your effect. You can spice up the reverb or delay with a soft chorus without altering the original signal. You can also pan the track to one side and its delay to the other - a nice touch] It opens up a whole new world of music production.

This is how you can use send effects in Cubase: First create an FX channel, name it appropriately and insert the desired effect into this channel.

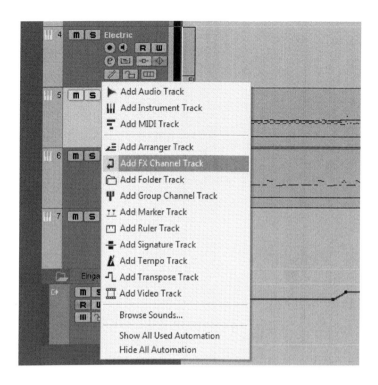

(Creating an FX Channel in Cubase)

Now go to the track that you would like to send to the FX channel and open its settings (that is, click on the "e" button). The left side of the EQ is where you usually place the effects. But this time turn your attention to the right side. There you can insert the FX channel you created.

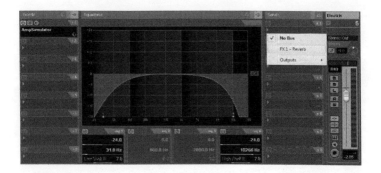

(Sending an Instrument to the FX channel)

Make sure to move the slider below the FX channel's name to the right, otherwise the track's signal will not reach the FX channel. Now you should be able to hear the reverb via the FX channel.

(Slider Moved to the Right, Pre-Fader Function Activated)

You might notice that right above the FX channel's name in the instrument settings there is a button to switch between post-fader and pre-fader, with post-fader being the default. What's the difference? In a post-fader send the output of the effect channel will vary in a proportional fashion to the output of the instrument. So if you decrease the instrument's volume level, the same will happen to the FX channel. In other words: the ratio of dry-to-wet is preserved in this case.

When choosing pre-fader you get full control over the output of the effect channel. Even when moving the instrument's volume fader all the way down to -∞, the output of the FX channel will remain unchanged. This is useful if you only want to listen to the processed signal and not the original signal that created it.

In A Nutshell - Reverb And Delay

- *The difference between reverb and delay is a result of how our brain processes sound.*

- *Reverb (= hall) is made up of sound wave reflections that are blended with the original sound, while delay (= echo) consists of distinctly perceived reflections.*

- *The reverb time is a measure of how long the sound persists. The larger the room, the longer the reverb time. 0.5 s for bedrooms, 1.5 s for concert halls.*

- *The pre-delay tells us how long it takes the first reflection to reach us. The farther we are from a reflecting wall, the longer the pre-delay.*

- *The diffusion parameter simulates surface roughness. For a rough surface (and thus warm and subtle reverb) set it close to 100 %.*

- *Don't use too much reverb or delay. Cut the low frequencies to avoid a muddy mix, cut the high frequencies to achieve a natural sound.*

- *Delay is the time between two reflections. It is usually necessary to synchronize it with your song's rhythm.*

- *Use reverb and delay to create a sense of depth. Vocals and solo instruments in the front, guitars and drums in the middle, everything else in the back.*

1.5. Gates

Gates are the audio engineer's waste disposal tool. They are not spectacular, but extremely useful. When a track is supposed to be silent but it is not, the (noise) gate will take care of it. Suppose for example that you are recording a vocal track. During pauses, a lot of background noises become audible: rumbling, heavy breathing, clearing the throat, etc ... While not particularly loud, they can still make a mix dirty. This might be fine for heavy metal, but not so much for pop, rock or classical music. Here's where the gate comes in.

A gate silences a track completely as long as its volume level is below a **threshold**. Once the threshold is reached, the gate becomes inactive and lets the audio pass. In the image below you can see what the workings of a gate look like. The original audio is at the top, the gated audio at the bottom.

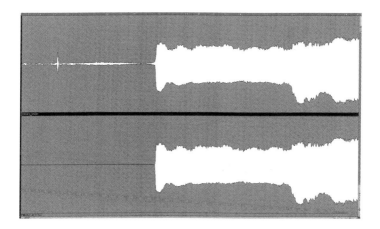

The noise that was in the track before the singer springs into action is now gone. Note that the threshold has to be chosen carefully. If it's too low, there is the danger of some noise coming through, if it's too high, the gate might cut out relevant audio signals. You have to find the right value by trial and error.

(The Noise Gate in Cubase)

What about the other parameters? Just like compressors, gates usually feature attack and release. The attack specifies how long it takes the gate to open. For drums and guitars very short attacks of around 1 ms work just fine. In case of vocals however, such a low value could lead to an overly abrupt end to the silence. To avoid this, choose a value closer to 10 ms for the lead and 50 ms for the backings. Typical values for the release are anywhere between 100 and 300 ms.

As for the hold, it is the minimum duration the gate stays open or closed. Some signals and thresholds might cause the gate to nervously open and close in rapid succession. The hold function brings calm into this by forcing the gate to remain in its current state for a while. As a reference, you can use 100 ms for drums and guitars and 250 ms for vocals.

In A Nutshell - Gates

- *Gates silence a track when it's supposed to be silent.*

- *Set the threshold to a value that mutes the background gibberish, but leaves the music intact.*

1.6. Chorus

In a perfect world, imperfection is king
(Anonymous)

Chorus (as well as other modulation effects such as flanger, phaser and tremolo) gained in popularity when a wave of psychedelic music swept across the globe in the sixties. While the music industry went back to more pragmatic tunes in the following decades, the modulation effects remained in use. Chorus is still among the most often used effects in music production, though today it is applied in a much more subtle manner.

- **Why Chorus?**

Before we look at how plugins create the chorus effect, let's take a look at the big picture. Suppose you record a solo violin and duplicate this track several times. Will the result sound like a violin section with several different violin players? No, unfortunately not. It will just sound like a solo track copied several times, which is not helpful. Is there any way we can get it to sound more like a real violin section?

This is what the chorus effect is for. Inserting it into the solo violin track will give the impression of having multiple violins playing rather than just one. So the **chor**us effect simulates a **choir** and produces a rich, thick and warm sound while doing so. No wonder it's the audio engineer's darling.

- **How It Works**

Suppose we mix a duplicate to a solo violin track and hit play. Why does the result not sound like two different violin players? The problem is that the duplicate fits the original track perfectly, they have exactly the same tempo and pitch at any time, while two real violin players would always be slightly off in timing and pitch. So to give the impression of more than one player, we need to modify the duplicate in a way that simulates this natural variation in timing and pitch.

Chorus plugins first create a duplicate of the track and "equip" the duplicate with a delay (not in the sense of echo, but in the sense of shifting the duplicate's starting point). To simulate variations in timing, the amount of delay varies with time. In fancy audio engineering terms: the delay time is modulated with an LFO, short for low frequency oscillator. A typical value for a chorus delay is around 20 milliseconds with variations of plus/minus 5 milliseconds. One side-effect of the modulation is that the pitch also varies with time, which completes the illusion of imperfect timing and pitch.

- **The Parameters**

(Basic Chorus Plugin in Cubase)

A parameter found in almost all chorus plugins is the **rate** (or speed). It determines at what frequency the delay time, and thus pitch, of the duplicate varies. In general it holds true that the higher the rate, the more pronounced the chorus effect is. For a subtle thickening, rates below 0.4 Hz work best. Many plugins also feature a sync-function to bring the delay time and pitch variations in line with the song's rhythm. This is neat, but not essential as we are used to hearing (natural) out-of-sync chorus effects in choirs and string sections.

The parameters **delay** (depending on plugin the initial or average delay time) and the **width** (a measure of the size of the delay time variations) give you additional control over the oscillations. Again we can go by the same rule of thumb: higher values result in a stronger chorus effect. To leave the effect in the background, keep the width below 10 %. Once the width goes past 40 %, the pitch variations of the duplicate can produce unpleasing dissonances, especially when combined with a high rate. Last but not least, the **spatial** parameter allows you to control the stereo width of the effect.

- **When To Use Chorus**

The tracks that make up the background layer of a song (strings, pads, background vocals and to a lesser extend rhythm guitars) are the perfect candidates for chorusing. With the right settings, the chorus effect will turn a relatively sparse background into a thick and soft layer.

As for the lead vocals, a little chorus might add some depth to a thin voice, but the effect should be applied as subtle as possible so that the natural sound of the voice remains intact.

An interesting variation is to apply the chorus effect only to certain phrases (for example the end of the refrain), giving the impression that other singers join in at lyric lines that are central to the song.

If you've got a bass line that is not moving too quickly and instead focuses on laying a stable foundation, you might want to add a nice oscillating effect to it using a low rate chorus. It is a nice way of making a somewhat static bass "come to life". We could go on and on, but it is much more instructive if I leave the experimenting up to you.

In A Nutshell - Chorus

- *The chorus effect simulates a choir. It gives the impression that multiple instruments are playing instead of just one.*

- *It is produced by creating a duplicate and delaying the duplicate by a varying amount. This also creates a varying pitch shift.*

- *Apply it in a subtle manner unless you are producing psychedelic music.*

- *Perfect for chorusing are the tracks that make up the background: background vocals, strings, pads and rhythm guitars.*

1.7. Other Effects

Unfortunately, it is not possible to have a look at all the fantastic audio effects that are out there. But there are a few more that deserve being mentioned and that might come in handy as you are working on optimizing your mix.

- **Exciters**

Exciters (also called enhancers) have an aura of mystery surrounding them. They are relatively new devices, first used in the seventies, and have been too expensive for home-recoding musicians and even small studios until the dawn of the digital age. Today high quality exciter plugins are available for as little as $ 250 (Aphex Vintage Aural Exciter) and there are even some freeware exciters out there that produce acceptable results (X-Cita by Elogoxa).

(X-cita Plugin)

When you add distortion to sound, a large number of high-frequency harmonics appear. This is just a natural process. However, these added harmonics are random and do not relate to the fundamental notes in your music. So the overall effect is rather dissonant. Exciters make sure that only the harmonics relevant to the music are kept, giving the sound an interesting and thick sparkle.

Try it out - your music might profit from this additional harmonic content, especially if there are a lot of (relatively lifeless) MIDI tracks in the mix. As always, keep it subtle and use it on individual instruments rather than the stereo output if possible. Too much "excitement" can quickly become harsh, unnatural and fatiguing.

- **Saturation**

In the 80s it took professional studios with expensive state-of-the-art equipment and top musicians to produce a clean and polished mix. With the rise of DAWs and VST instruments, producing clean audio has become a lot cheaper. Is this a happy end? Depends on who you ask. Many producers and music enthusiasts claim that today's music is too clean and too cold. They miss the "dirty" warmth analog audio devices forced onto a song.

If you feel the same way, you will be happy to hear that with the help of saturation plugins you can revive the good ol' analog sound. They accomplish this task by adding soft distortion and non-linear compression to the mix, both effects that are very typical for audio playback on tube or tape devices. Many audio engineers use saturation in the mastering phase, applying the effect in a subtle fashion across the entire mix to glue it together.

A popular saturation plugin for mastering purposes is Vintage Warmer by PSP ($ 150). For those who just want to try out the effect or are on a tight budget, there are freeware alternatives such as FerrisTDS by the audio blogger Variety Of Sound. The presets allow you to jump right in and see what fits your music.

(FerrisTDS Plugin)

1.8. Automation

To improve is to change; to be perfect is to change often.
(Winston Churchill)

Another great tool for getting the most out of your mix is automation. It can smoothen a track, bring life to a cold and machine-like MIDI instrument, optimize the dynamics of a song and create neat special effects. The possibilities are endless. So if you haven't used automation before, make sure to include it in your toolbox in the future.

- **The Principle**

When you choose the volume of a track, it remains at this level throughout the entire song. Same goes for the pan position of the track, the gain of your EQ cut, the mix level of the reverb, the bypass setting of the exciter, and so on. Once chosen, it will remain unchanged for the duration of the mix. But this does not need to be.

Almost all DAWs offer the possibility to use any parameter as a variable. You can achieve a smooth instrument fade-in by automating its volume level, have the instrument wander across the stereo field by automating the pan position, make an EQ cut more pronounced as the hook begins by automating the EQ's gain parameter, and so on. You can make almost any parameter time-dependent, the only limit is your time and imagination.

In Cubase using automation is as simple as activating the **write** button of a track and doing all the desired changes while playing back the song. The changes you make will be saved in separate automation tracks (one track for each parameter that was altered during the playback). You can always come back to the automation tracks at a later point to edit them. To open the automation tracks of an audio track, right click on the audio track and select "Show Used Automation".

Sometimes I activate the write function and do a random change on a parameter just to create the corresponding automation track. Then I put in the desired automation manually, which is usually more precise than recording the changes during playback. Make sure to activate the **read** button when playing the song after you put in the changes. Otherwise the automation will not be read.

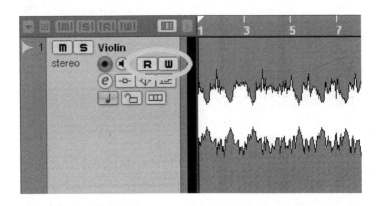

(A Track's Read And Write Buttons)

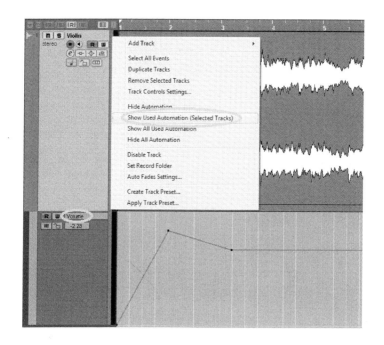

(Opening Automation Track, Example Of Automated Volume Level)

- **Some Inspiration**

As mentioned, the possibilities are endless. So we limit ourselves here to listing a few ideas for inspiration. Some are subtle and serve to smoothen or widen a mix, others are very much noticeable and can be used as special effects when appropriate.

Volume:

- [Fade-ins and fade-outs of individual tracks for a more smooth sound. Also helps in embedding the tracks in the mix.]

- Cross-fade two tracks, that is, have the one fade-out while the other fades in. Often used to overlap two simultaneous lyric lines in a song or merge different recording takes in a more natural fashion.

- Make the beginning of a solo louder to grab the listener's attention.

- Emphasize specific parts of a song such as the chorus, bridge or interlude.

Panning:

- Pan background tracks wider in the chorus.

- Have a track move across the stereo field (if you'd like to hear an example of this, check out the guitar at the beginning Meat Loaf's "I'd Do Anything For Love").

- Have a track move to the side as it fades out to underline the volume automation.

EQ:

- Boost the lower midrange during parts in which only a few instruments are active (for example: intro) for a warm and full sound.

- Have the lead vocals sound like they are coming through a telephone during the bridge. Grabs the listener's attention and gives variety to the sound. To achieve a telephone sound, cut everything below 800 Hz and above 3.000 Hz and boost everything in between until distortions appear. The boost should be at maximum level at around 1.500 Hz.

Effects:

- Emphasize individual words in the lyrics with reverb, delay, distortion, etc ... to underline their importance to the message.

- Turn up the mix parameter of your effects during the chorus to have it really stand out.

2. Mixing

2.1. The Big Picture

The whole is more than the sum of its parts.
(Aristotle)

Up to now, all we've been doing is learning about the effects that are commonly applied in music production and how to automate tracks. Now that we are familiar with that, it's time to get to business. You've written the song, recorded all the tracks (or created the MIDI file or both) and imported whatever needs to be imported into the DAW. This is where the mixing phase begins. The ultimate goal of mixing is to turn the separate tracks into a homogenous, three-dimensional mix.

What constitutes a good mix? Ask ten audio engineers and you'll get twenty answers. Each musician and audio engineer has his or her own idea about what a good mix should sound like. That's why we'll restrict the following list to common denominators - elements that most musicians and audio engineers would name as characteristics of a good mix.

- **Clarity:** Despite aiming for a homogenous mix, each instrument should be clearly heard. You don't want the bass and kick merging into a boomy "something". In a good mix, your ears will be able to locate the bass and kick as separate parts.

- **Multi-Dimensionality**: Being able to locate an instrument in the mix means perceiving it as being in its own space. A good mix should give the illusion that some instruments are to the left, some to the right, some in the front and some in the back.

- **Balance:** A good mix should have left-right balance as well as spectral balance. The latter means that the different frequency bands (such as bass, lower mids, upper mids, air) should be in a natural or pleasing proportion. You don't want the bass overpowering everything else.

- **Emphasis**: The hook of a song should be catchy and sound well without the use of hoity toity mixing and mastering tricks. This is the songwriter's job. But in a good mix, the hook is emphasized by all means appropriate - effects, automation, dynamic variation.

- **Finalized**: Yes, the mastering phase will follow. But it is only meant to polish a completed mix in which all problems are taken care of. Mastering does not turn a flat mix into a great one. The mix should already sound spectacular on its own.

- **Headroom:** During the mastering phase it might be necessary to apply some EQ changes or subtle effects. A good mix doesn't peak above - 4 dB, thus leaving enough dynamic space for the final polishing. Don't worry about optimizing loudness, this is part of the mastering stage.

Make sure to understand and remember each of these elements. Try your best to "make them happen" in your mix by applying what you've learned about effects and automation as well as the mixing strategy that will be laid out in this chapter.

2.2. Mixing Strategy

Details create the big picture.
(Sanford I. Weill)

- **The Mixing Space**

Mixing is a very individual process, there's no default mixing chain we can go through to arrive at the best mix possible. What works for one genre, might fail in another. So it's important to keep an open mind and adopt what produces the most pleasing results for your genre, your style and your perspective on music. Accordingly, the following mixing strategy should be taken as a suggestion rather than a set of axioms written in stone.

To understand the idea behind this mixing strategy, picture a three-dimensional coordinate system in your mind. It has two axis that spawn the flat ground and one height axis. One of the two ground axis symbolizes the left-right direction, while the other represents depth. The height axis stands for the frequency range. Our job is to **assign each track in our mix a more or less isolated region in the mixing space**.

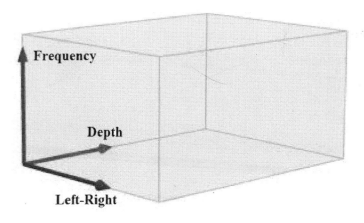

(Three-Dimensional Mixing Space)

Consider for example a rhythm guitar that is panned 40 % to the right, is in the background of the mix and ranges from 80 - 5.000 Hz. These three pieces of information locate the rhythm guitar in our mixing space. When adding another track to it, we want to minimize overlapping. For example, a bass that is panned to the center, is in the front of the mix and ranges from 40 - 5.000 Hz might come in conflict with the rhythm guitar. While sufficiently separated in left-right and depth direction, the frequency overlap might force us to make sacrifices by applying EQ cuts.

On the other hand, if we add another guitar that also ranges from 80 - 5.000 Hz, EQ cuts won't do the trick anymore since the overlapping region is so large (complementary cuts might still be a good idea though). Here we have to take other means of separation: pan it 40 % to the left for example and/or put it in the middle of the mix. Whatever we decide to do, it should serve the ultimate goal: minimize left-right, depth and frequency overlapping.

This approach to mixing might seem unnecessarily abstract at first, but it is a great way to achieve clarity, multi-dimensionality and left-right balance at the same time. Of course you don't have memorize all the frequency ranges for this to work. To minimize frequency overlaps it is sufficient to know that the combination of certain instruments (bass and kick, bass and guitar, guitar and cymbals) might force you to make some cuts.

- **Step By Step**

You should include the most important effects on the individual tracks before you start separating them. Including them at a later point might force you to rethink the instrument's place in the mix and then you might end up reorganizing all the tracks. So if you want a chorus on the rhythm guitar, **insert the effect at the very beginning. Same goes for the volume level** of the tracks. Set them early on to have the "big picture".

Once you roughly set the volume levels, inserted the effects and assigned all the tracks their proper region in the mixing space, you can move on to **spectral balancing** and **automation** (for example to emphasize the hook and smoothen transitions). Balancing the spectral bands can be as easy as adjusting some volume faders or as complex as using a multi-band compressor - whatever seems appropriate. Last but not least, do some **troubleshooting** if necessary. This should finalize the mix.

Here's the summary of the mixing strategy:

1. Import Reference Track

2. Roughly Set Volume Levels

3. Insert Effects On Tracks

4. Separate Tracks By Frequency, Depth and Left-Right

5. Spectral Balancing

6. Automation

7. Troubleshooting

Troubleshooting does not have to be postponed till the end. If you notice a problem, take care of it as soon as you can as not to drag it along or (even worse) end up pronouncing it during the mixing process. The final troubleshoot is there to guarantee that no problems spill into the mastering phase.

You might have noticed that there's one point we haven't talked about yet: the **reference track**. When mixing, it is easy to get lost in details or lose sight of an overpowering bass. That's why it's important to switch to a fully mixed and mastered song from time to time. It will help you to notice problems you might have already gotten used to while working on your mix. Which song to choose as reference? It could be a hit song from your genre that has the sound you'd like to achieve or one of your earlier mixes that turned out really well.

- **Final Remarks**

Never forget to **take breaks**. While the reference track helps a lot in avoiding tunnel vision (or rather tunnel hearing), it does not make you immune to it. Never try to finish a mix in one continuous session. Get a rough mix ready, then sleep on it or at least have a coffee break and watch an episode of "The Simpsons". If there's still something off in the mix, you'll immediately hear it when you get back to the mix after a long break.

Before you take a break, you might want to spend a few minutes creating **alternate versions**. If you think the song could profit from softer vocals, export a "vocals soft" mix. If the idea of a more aggressive guitar intrigues you, save a "guitar sharp" mix. This is the time to experiment and when you resume the mixing session, these alternative versions will be very helpful in guiding you into the right direction.

If you mix a song that was not written or performed by you, it is a good idea **not to involve the songwriters or the performing band too closely** in the mixing process. For one, it is likely that they are not willing to make the sacrifices necessary to create a clear mix. Also, each band member might insist on having his or her instrument emphasized without taking into account the big picture.

So instead of mixing as a team, interview the songwriters or band members to understand their vision of the song and make a rough mix by yourself. After the rough mix is complete, ask for revision requests and finalize the mix (or make another rough mix) according to those. This approach is a good compromise between the vision of the artists and their very subjective perspective on how to achieve it during mixing.

2.3. Separating Tracks

Equality and separation cannot exist in the same space.
(Jason Mraz)

Roughly setting the volume levels and inserting the effects, the first two steps in our mixing strategy, need no further explanation at this point as the basic tips on using effects were included in chapter one. However, we will elaborate a bit on separating the tracks.

Our goal is to separate the tracks by frequency, depth and left-right. In this order? Yes, in this order. Separating by left-right is as simple as turning the pan knob. If you start with this (most obvious) step, conflicts due to frequency overlapping and depth will become less noticeable, especially to the untrained ear. So start with the least obvious steps and try to achieve a pleasing separation before you begin to turn the pan knob. This will help you to get the most out of the space available to your mix.

- **Frequency**

You've got a lot of tracks in your mix but only one audible frequency band (spanning from 16 - 20.000 Hz), so manage wisely and be willing to make sacrifices to prevent ending up with a muddy mess. The most common conflicts as well as ways to prevent them have been mentioned in the Quick Tips section in chapter 1.3.

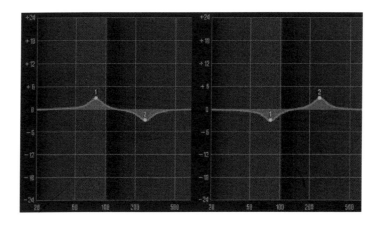

(Complementary Cuts: Left Kick EQ, Right Bass EQ)

- **Depth**

To find out how a sense of depth can be introduced in a mix, let's take a look at how sound waves change as they travel through air. Ideally, a wave front forms a sphere around the sound source. As the sound waves propagate, this sphere grows. This means that the initial energy contained in the wave front is spread over an ever-increasing surface area and accordingly, the loudness of the sound waves decreases. So, no surprise here, distance sources are at a **lower volume level**. This is so obvious that many tend to forget that volume is a great way to underline depth. Just for reference: if the distance doubles, the volume goes down by 6 dB.

Another obvious effect is that the sound of distant sources reaches us a little later. Since sound travels at around 330 meters per second at room temperature, this means that for every meter distance there's a **delay** (not in the sense of echo) of 3 milliseconds compared to sources that are right next to us. So if the drummer is located five meters behind the guitarist, the drum sound will reach us 15 milliseconds later. Use the info bar of an audio event for precise shifting. This works for both audio and MIDI tracks. For MIDI tracks you can also the "MIDI Modifiers" effect to shift the track. Just by the way: this effect is also very helpful in making MIDI instruments sound more realistic by introducing random variations in position, pitch, velocity and length.

(Info Bar In Cubase With Event Start Location Highlighted)

("MIDI Modifiers" Effect In Cubase)

Then there's the uneven absorption of frequencies by air. As already mentioned, air dampens higher frequencies more strongly than lower frequencies. So air acts like a low-pass filer as it transmits sound waves. The greater the distance to a source, the stronger the **high-cut** should be.

Sound coming from a source at great distance generally contains less direct sound and more reflected sound. You can simulate this in a DAW by turning up the mix and diffusion parameter in the **reverb** plugin. Of course making the delay (in the sense of echo) more noticeable works just as well. Other plugins can also help in creating more depth, among them **chorus** as well as other modulation effects, which all tend to push a track in the background.

Here's a summary of how to add depth to a track:

1. Lower The Volume

2. Shift The Signal's Starting Point Slightly

3. Apply A High-Cut

4. Increase Mix And Diffusion In Reverb

5. Add Chorus

- **Left-Right**

Once frequency conflicts are taken care of and the instruments are "equipped" with some depth, it's time to turn the pan knob. This will no doubt be the most noticeable way of getting some distance between the individual tracks. But where to pan which instrument? This is mostly up to you and your song, but there are some things worth keeping in mind.

Always keep **low frequency instruments** such as the bass, kick, cello and dark pads close to the center. There are two good reasons for this. Firstly, the bass band contains most of the energy in a mix and it thus makes sense to distribute the load evenly between the two speakers. This also makes it easier to achieve left-right balance later on. Secondly, bass-heavy sound sources are generally more difficult to locate and are perceived as coming from the center even if they aren't there. So only pan bass instruments by more than 15 % if there's a really good reason to do so. One more thing to keep in mind: since we've decided to leave the kick in the center, it wouldn't make much sense to pan other **drum tracks** widely (unless for artistic reasons). For a natural sound we need to keep them in the vicinity of the kick.

Another track that is usually kept right in the center is the **main vocal line**. It is, after all, a central element of your song and this way of panning just underlines its importance. As for the **background vocals**, they are traditionally panned very widely to encompass the entire mix. This works great if you've got multiple background vocals and thus the opportunity to distribute them left and right. But what if there's only one? In this case it's wise to go easier on the panning and find a way to balance the background vocal track with another background instrument. Alternatively, you can double the background vocal track and use the duplicate for balance.

With the low frequency instruments, drum tracks and main vocals in the center, the center is already quite crowded. So whatever additional instruments you have, keep them away from the center (exception: a **solo guitar** that takes over for the main vocals during an interlude). For example, if there's a pad and a rhythm guitar in your mix, pan the one 50 % left and the other 50 % right. This way there's enough space for each track and the mix should be fairly balanced.

Avoid panning instruments to the exact same spot. Though there are a lot of instruments close to the center, there's always the possibility of getting a few percent between them. Make use of that, a few percent can make a big difference. Also, panning completely left or right often sounds very unnatural. **Avoid such extreme settings** unless this is part of your grand plan.

While panning, **keep an eye out for imbalances**. The meters for the left and right output should always go to about the same height. This is true for all parts of the song, so check them separately. Even when you made sure that the combination of all tracks together (for example during the final chorus) produces a balanced mix, there might still be balance issues during parts with only a few active tracks (such as the intro, verse or interlude). To avoid this, start the panning session with the more laid back parts of the song.

A nice way to get some more distance between the instruments without resorting to extreme panning or too much loss of spectral content are **stereo enhancers**. They can produce a spectacular stereo image with very little work. A disadvantage though is that most stereo enhancers also spread the bass instruments (which we want to keep centered). So apply with care or better yet, use the mid-side technique, that is introduced in the next chapter, to improve the stereo image. It might be more work, but will result in a cleaner mix.

(Stereo Enhancer in Cubase)

Here's a summary of the panning principles:

1. Low Frequency Instruments In The Center

2. Main Vocals And Solo Instruments In The Center

3. Wide Panning Of Background Vocals

4. Avoid Panning To The Exact Same Spot

5. Avoid Extreme Panning

6. Create Left-Right Balance

7. Use Stereo Enhancer Or M/S For More Stereo

3. Mastering

3.1. Basic Idea

A rolling stone gathers no moss, but it gains a certain polish.
(Oliver Herford)

Many people overestimate the impact of mastering on a song's characteristic sound. Establishing the sound and fixing all the problems is the job of the mixing phase. Mastering just **gives the song a little polish, enhances its loudness and optimizes it from a technical point of view**. Accordingly, you should focus most of your energy and time (90 % or more) on mixing and leave as little as possible up to mastering.

If the mix is bad, mastering will not change this. It will make the song louder and more compatible, but not better. In this case going back to mixing is the only sensible choice. If the mix is fantastic on its own, you can and should limit the mastering phase to optimizing loudness. The "full mastering package" should only be applied to a good mix that is still lacking a bit of punch or has minimal balance issues.

Mastering usually refers to **editing the stereo out**, so during this phase you won't have access to individual tracks. You cannot make an instrument louder or alter its pan position. Whatever changes you make will be applied across the mix. To not destroy a good mix, all changes (except the loudness increase) must be subtle.

Note that what many nowadays refer to as mastering (the process of giving the song a final polish) was once called pre-mastering by audio engineers. Before the age of digital DAWs, mastering meant creating the physical copy (glass master) of the already polished song that would serve as the model for producing further physical copies.

(A Glass Master - The Holy Grail Of Analog Music)

3.2. Mastering Strategy

However beautiful the strategy, you should occasionally look at the results
(Winston Churchill)

Suppose we have a mix that is good, but in need of a little bit of mastering. What to do? As always, there's no single answer. But in mastering there's much more agreement than in mixing. The strategies and the order in which the steps are taken are often quite similar. So what you find below is a rather typical mastering chain, but by no means the only possibility.

Remember that the mastering process is supposed to guarantee the **maximum amount of compatibility** with different playback devices. So it is vital that you work with all the equipment available to you. Listen to the song on your loudspeakers, your headphones, your car radio, your television and even the cell phone when mastering. Note the problems that come up on the respective devices and try to get rid of them without changing the song's character or introducing new problems. Make sure to deactivate all functions that alter the playback (bass boost, loudness, stereo).

Another thing to watch out for is the **"louder is better" trap** and I'm not referring to the loudness war here. For some odd psychological reasons, we have a hard time judging a change that increases or decreases the overall loudness. We tend to believe that it must be better because it's louder. This is why when applying a compressor, I always choose the make-up gain in a way that will leave the overall volume unchanged to get a fair comparison.

1. Reference Track

Again the first step should be importing a song into your DAW that is well-mastered and representative of your genre. Compare from time to time to stay on track.

2. EQ

In mastering the EQ is used to remove the sub-bass, to get rid of awkward resonances, to establish spectral balance or just to sweeten the mix. To keep the changes subtle, make sure to stick to wide, low gain boosts or cuts. If a problem only appears in the left or right channel, feel free to make the necessary EQ incision only in the respective channel. As long as the incision is not too extreme, this shouldn't cause any balance issues.

3. Peak-Limiting

If there are excessive peaks in your music that are likely to cause trouble later on, this is the time to remove them using a limiter with a well-chosen threshold (output). To catch all the peaks without removing relevant content you probably have to apply the limiter part by part.

Make sure not to limit too strongly at this point. For one, a compressor and another limiter will be applied at later stages in the mastering process, further dampening the peaks. Also, don't forget that peaks are an integral part of a natural sound. If you remove them mercilessly, the result will be a strangely flat mix offering few surprises.

4. Glueing

In this phase you can apply effects to make the mix more homogeneous. This could mean including a hardly noticeable reverb to put the mix in a shared room or some saturation for nostalgic effect. Exciters might work as well, but must be applied carefully since they have a significant impact on the sound.

5. Compressing

Applying the compressor will make the mix more dense and prepare it for loudness optimization. If the frequency bands are well-balanced and the song only requires little compression, a single-band compressor should be your first choice. If on the other hand there are still spectral balance issues or a harder compression is desired, consider using a multi-band compressor instead. For genres that naturally have a large dynamic range (such as orchestral or acoustic music), give the parallel compression technique a try.

6. Automation

This stage offers you one last opportunity to put the parts of the song in the right proportion in terms of volume and add some special effects such as wider stereo in the chorus.

7. Master-Limiting

Now comes the loudness optimization. Use a limiter (or a maximizer) to push the volume to the desired level. Typical peak volume levels for a pop or rock song after mastering are - 6 dB in the intro or interlude, - 3 dB in the verse and close to 0 dB in the chorus and solo. Play it safe and don't go beyond - 0.3 dB as this might cause problems on older playback systems. In the image below you can see an example audio track before and after loudness optimization using Cubase's Maximizer plugin.

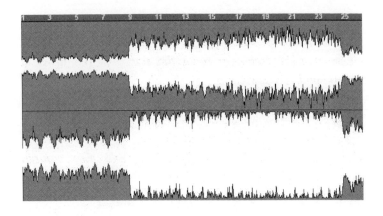

Additionally to pushing volume, the final limiter also prevents clipping and the distortions associated with it. This of course means that at this point we cannot make any further changes that will have an impact on the song's dynamics. If we do, we lose the protection of the limiter. It must be last in line to properly serve as a "brick-wall".

8. Dithering And Export

Up to now you will (or should) have been working in 24 or 32 bit. If your final mix is meant to go on a CD, you have to export the mastered song in 16 bit. To minimize quantization noise during this conversion, add dither to the mix before exporting.

Background Info - Digitization

*To be able to store and alter a signal in a computer, we have to transform a continuous analog signal into a series of zeros and ones. This process called digitization. It is broken down in two steps: **sampling** and **quantization**.*

During sampling, the analog signal is measured at regular time intervals. For example, a sampling rate of 44.1 kHz means that the computer reads the signal 44.100 times in one second. To sample a signal without data loss (that is, without changing relevant parts of its spectrum in the process), the sampling rate needs to be at least twice the highest frequency in the signal. Hence, a sampling rate of 44.1 kHz is sufficient to digitize signals that contain frequencies of 22.050 Hz and below (which is well past the threshold of hearing for any age).

During the next step, the continuous signal values (voltage or amplitude) are rounded to a grid of fixed values. This is called quantization. Each of the fixed values is represented by a line of zeros and ones. In a system with an x bit word size, the grid will contain 2^x values. For example, a 16-bit system allows 65.536 fixed values. So the higher the word size, the finer the grid and the smaller the errors that result from rounding the voltage or amplitude of the analog signal.

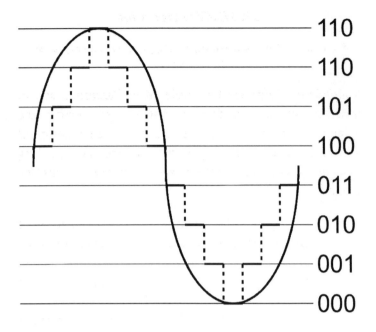

110

110

101

100

011

010

001

000

(A sine wave and its digitized form in a 3-bit system)

The quantization errors are usually not audible in systems with 16-bit (or higher). But even at these word sizes problems can occur for signals that are very soft. In this case the amplitude is in the order of the quantization step and thus forcing the signal onto the grid severely distorts it, resulting in "granular noise". Dithering, the process of adding very weak random noise to the signal, helps to reduce the quantization noise.

3.3. Mid/Side Processing

Stay committed to your decisions, but stay flexible in your approach.
(Tony Robbins)

Mid/Side (in short: M/S) mastering is an interesting way of approaching the mix from a different perspective and gaining access to parts of the music that are usually not accessible during mastering. It has been around for a long time, but gained significantly in popularity over the past ten years.

Commonly we think of a stereo mix as being composed of one left (L) and one right (R) channel. However, this is not the only possible way to break down a stereo signal. We can also construct it using the so-called **sum** (S) on the one hand and the **difference** (D) on the other. The sum is what we get when we combine the left and right channel into a mono mix. It contains all the signals that are identical in the left and right channel, that is, all signals that appear at the same time with the same volume in both channels.

L + R = S

The left-overs are the signals that differ in the left and right channel. They make up the difference. We get the difference by combining the left channel with the phase-inverted right channel into a mono mix.

L + (-R) = D

Here's how you can do it in Cubase. First, import the mix that you'd like to split up in a sum and difference. Make sure to select "split channels" during import so that you have access to the left and right channels separately.

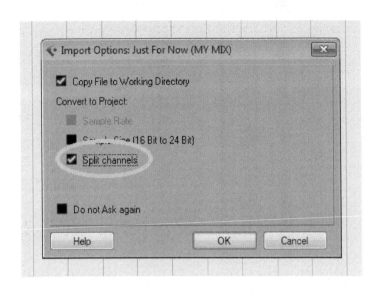

Now you should see both channels in front of you. Creating the sum is easy. Go to "File", "Export" and "Audio Mixdown". Export the mix after selecting "Mono-Export".

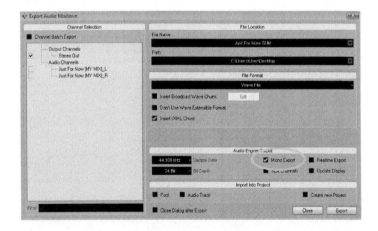

Important note: the volume of the left and right channel will add during the mixdown. So to avoid clipping you have to lower the volume level of the stereo out. Lower it by - 6 dB to be on the safe side.

Now that we have the sum (or mid signal), let's create the difference. Exit the "Audio Mixdown" form and open the mixer (F3). In the mixer you can phase-invert the right channel with the simple click of a button. Just above the pan slider you should see a circle with a straight line going through it. Activate this button to phase-invert the channel.

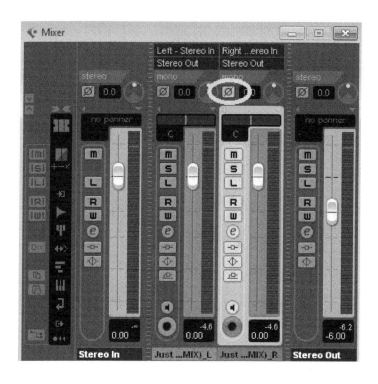

With this done, go back to the "Audio Mixdown" form, check "Mono-Export" and export. Now we also have the difference (or side signal). Import both the sum and difference into your project. It's a good idea to keep the left and right channels as well for comparison. Just mute them if you don't use them.

We'll split the difference up a little further. Duplicate the difference track. Pan the original difference track hard to the left, phase-invert the other difference track and pan it hard to the right. Now you should have five tracks in your project: the muted left and right channels, the sum, the difference panned to the left and the difference panned to the right and phase-inverted.

Here's a summary of the process:

1. Import Mix, Select "split channels"

2. Mono-Export → Sum

3. Phase-Invert Right Channel

4. Mono-Export → Difference

5. Import Sum And Difference

6. Duplicate Difference Track

7. Pan Original Left, Pan Phase-Inverted Duplicate Right

So now instead of mastering using the left and right channels (or the simple stereo sum of the two), we are free to alter the sum and difference of the signal. How can we use this to improve the song? One important advantage of M/S processing is that it gives us **straight-forward control over the stereo image**. Widening and narrowing the stereo is as simple as increasing or decreasing the volume level of the difference tracks.

Of course changing the volume of difference signals is not the only way to sculpt the stereo image. In principle, everything goes as long as it produces a pleasing sound. We can add reverb or delay to stretch the difference tracks, soften them using chorus, add harmonies using the exciter, etc ...

The M/S technique also provides the means to create a true **mono bass**. As we learned in the previous chapter, there are good reasons to keep instruments with lots of low frequency content in the center. But even if we pan them to the center, there will be some bass left in the difference signal. To get rid of these bass signals, simply apply a highpass filter to the difference tracks.

When applying **compressors** to the M/S mix, it is common to compress the sum more strongly (lower threshold, higher ratio) than the difference. This has several positive effects. The sum, which acts as the foundation of the mix, becomes more stable and the stereo image widens as the loudness of the song increases. Hence it goes from relatively narrow in the soft parts (such as intro or interlude) to much wider during loud parts (chorus).

3.4. Don't Give Up

Don't give up before the miracle happens.
(Fannie Flagg)

You keenly read this book and carefully applied all the tips and strategies. Yet, you feel there's something missing. The mix simply doesn't sound as "punchy" and "in your face" as you hoped it would. Or even worse: it sounds like a mess. What happened? Experience happened. Or rather: lack thereof.

Mixing and mastering at a competitive level takes a lot of experience. You have to fall into the traps to notice them and to find out how to avoid them in the future. You have to train your ears to be able to spot problems and imbalances. You have to absorb the knowledge to remove said problems and imbalances without creating new problems. All of this takes time and a ton of horribly mixed and mastered songs.

Don't give up, this is where everyone starts, even a mixing and mastering god such as Bob Katz. Your songs will improve with time, it's a sure thing. How long does it take to reach a competitive level? This depends on how much you want it and how much time you are able to invest. I've seen people go from "meh" to "spectacular" within several months. All it takes is a vivid interest in the subject, a willingness to learn the basics and a lot of (not necessarily successful) mixing and mastering sessions.

4. Appendix

4.1. Calculating Frequencies

Though not vital for mixing and mastering, it is often helpful to know the exact frequencies of a fundamental and its overtones. Let n denote the number of half-steps from the chamber pitch (note A at 440 Hz) to the note we are interested in, with n being negative if the note is lower than the chamber pitch and positive if it is higher. Then the fundamental frequency of said note is:

$$F = 440 \cdot 2^{n/12}$$

The frequencies of the overtones are simple multiples of the fundamental frequency:

$$f_k = k \cdot F$$

with k = 2 for the first overtone, k = 3 for the second overtone, and so on. Let's go through an example on how to apply these formulas. Suppose we want to know the fundamental frequency corresponding to the middle C on the piano as well the frequency of the first few overtones. The middle C is three half-steps (A#, B, C) above the chamber pitch. Hence n = 3. So the frequency of the fundamental is:

$$F = 440 \cdot 2^{3/12} \approx 523 \ Hz$$

The overtones lie at:

$$f_2 = 2 \cdot 523 = 1046 \ Hz$$

$$f_3 = 3 \cdot 523 = 1569 \ Hz$$

$$f_4 = 4 \cdot 523 = 2092 \ Hz$$

4.2. Decibel

A way of expressing a quantity in relative terms is to do the ratio with respect to a reference value. This helps to put a quantity into perspective. For example, in mechanics the acceleration is often expressed in relation to the gravitational acceleration. Instead of saying the acceleration is 22 m/s^2 (which is hard to relate to unless you know mechanics), we can also say the acceleration is 22 / 9.81 $\approx$ 2.2 times the gravitational acceleration or simply 2.2 g's (which is much easier to comprehend).

The decibel (dB) is also **a general way of expressing a quantity in relative terms**, sort of a "logarithmic ratio". And just like the ratio, it is not a physical unit or limited to any field such as mechanics, audio, etc ... You can express any quantity in decibels. For example, if we take the reference value to be the gravitational acceleration, the acceleration 22 m/s^2 corresponds to 3.5 dB.

To calculate the decibel value L of a quantity x relative to the reference value x_0, we can use this formula:

$$L = 10 \cdot \log_{10}\left(\frac{x}{x_0}\right)$$

In acoustics the decibel is used to express the sound pressure level (SPL), measured in Pascal = Pa, using the threshold of hearing (0.00002 Pa) as reference. However, in this case a factor of twenty instead of ten is used. The change in factor is a result of inputting the squares of the pressure values rather than the linear values.

$$L = 20 \cdot \log_{10}\left(\frac{SPL}{0.00002}\right)$$

The sound coming from a stun grenade peaks at a sound pressure level of around 15,000 Pa. In decibel terms this is:

$$L = 20 \cdot \log_{10}\left(\frac{15,000}{0.00002}\right) \approx 178\, dB$$

which is way past the threshold of pain that is around 63.2 Pa (130 dB). Here are some typical values to keep in mind:

0 dB → Threshold of Hearing

20 dB → Whispering

60 dB → Normal Conversation

80 dB → Vacuum Cleaner

110 dB → Front Row at Rock Concert

130 dB → Threshold of Pain

160 dB → Bursting Eardrums

Why use the decibel at all? Isn't the ratio good enough for putting a quantity into perspective? The ratio works fine as long as the quantity doesn't go over many order of magnitudes. This is the case for the speeds or accelerations that we encounter in our daily lives. But when a quantity varies significantly and spans many orders of magnitude (which is what the SPL does), the decibel is much more handy and relatable.

Another reason for using the decibel for audio signals is provided by the Weber-Fechner law. It states that a stimulus is perceived in a logarithmic rather than linear fashion. So expressing the SPL in decibels can be regarded as a first approximation to how loud a sound is perceived by a person as opposed to how loud it is from a purely physical point of view.

Note that when combining two or more sound sources, the decibel values are not simply added. Rather, if we combine two sources that are equally loud and in phase, the volume increases by 6 dB (if they are out of phase, it will be less). For example, when adding two sources that are at 50 dB, the resulting sound will have a volume of 56 dB (or less).

4.3. Copyright and Disclaimer

Made in the USA
Columbia, SC
20 July 2019